# THINNING GRAPES

## MARY SHEEPSHANKS

**Fighting Cock Press**

First Published 1992 by The National Poetry Foundation
This Edition Published 2001 by Fighting Cock Press
Reprinted 2005 by Fighting Cock Press

**Fighting Cock Press:**
45 Middlethorpe Drive
York
YO24 1NA

Editor: Pauline Kirk
Consultant: Mabel Ferrett
Marketing: John Ferrett
Technical Advisor: Geoff Kirk

Printed by Peepal Tree Press
Cover Design by Graham Rust
Original Fighting Cock Logo by Stanley Chapman

ISBN 090674 21 0

*For James*

## *Acknowledgements*

Acknowledgements are due to the following:

**Journals**:

*Aireings, Caduceus, Christian, Envoi, Farmers Weekly, Foolscap, Network, Outposts, Pause, Pennine Platform, The New Welsh Review, The Times, Weyfarers*

**Anthologies**:

*Windfall* – Edited by Peggie Poole and Alison Chisholm
'James's Song' first appeared in *Vicky – A Bridge Between Two Worlds* by Ursula Burton, published by Darton Longman and Todd
and has been set to music by Paul Dutton

'Borrowed Time', 'Clowning', 'Cradle-Song', 'Gateways', 'Left-hand Gloves' and 'Why Were You Born?', appeared in:
*The Bird of My Loving* by Mary Sheepshanks, published by Penguin Books
*Blackthorn* has been set to music by Caroline McCausland
'Cradle-Song' won the Ivy James Memorial Prize 1992

### *Also by Mary Sheepshanks*

FICTION
*A Price for Everything,* 1995
*Facing the Music,* 1996
*Picking up the Pieces,* 1997
*Off Balance,* 2000
*The Venetian House*, 2005 (writing as Mary Nickson)
Published in the UK by Century/Arrow

NON FICTION
*The Bird of My Loving (A Personal Response to Loss and Grief)* 1997, published by Michael Joseph /Penguin Books

POETRY
*Patterns in the Dark,* 1991
2002 edition published by Fighting Cock Press
(First published by The National Poetry Foundation 1991)
*Kingfisher Days,* 1998, published by Fighting Cock Press
*Dancing Blues to Skylarks*, 2004, published by Fighting Cock Press

# CONTENTS

# Gateways
*(for Kenneth Parkinson)*

Some people seek
a holy place to pray,
or meditate, legs crossed
eyes shuttered, spirits far away,
touching tranquillity
through upturned palms;

but others like
to lean upon a gate
and let the sun's arm
rest across their backs;
watch circus swallows,
skimming farmyard stacks,
meticulously time their
aerobatic skills
while shadows murmur
mantras on far hills.

Long green diminuendos then
fluted by hidden willow-wrens
shall be a bell, an evensong, a psalm

– to each their individual
source of calm.

## Clowning

Slap on white greasepaint
Pagliacci's disguise
to keep anguish hidden
from curious eyes.

Stick a joke in your hatband
spray stars on your hair
laughter's the clothing
to cover despair.

One dress to the cleaners
sponge off any pain
grief is like gravy
if spilt it can stain.

## Al Fresco

*('Rest on the flight to Egypt' by Jan Breughel)*

A tapestry of flowers, a woodland grove
tame unicorns, a guinea pig or two
sunshine *and* shade...

they had it made!

No wonder that the baby grew to be
a handy chap at barbecues and weddings
quite a dab with fish kebabs
an ace at multiplying baps...
a good wine buff?
Well just with local stuff.

They picked the perfect picnic place
miraculous to do:
but then it must be easier, by far,
to stop a man who leads a donkey
than one who drives a car.

## A Farewell Gift
*(To Peggy McCausland)*

Because I shall not visit you again
I wish to bring you something beautiful,
a small but precious gift;
nothing extravagant or rich:
the cost of presents should be in the giving.

But what to give a traveller
who anticipates
a journey of the spirit,
sits, poised as an autumn swallow
on a telegraph wire
preparing to take wing?
Perhaps you too are waiting to migrate
to somewhere you have been before
and spend a season there
before return;

and will you congregate again
with those you love,
exchange experiences, teach and learn?
Eternal rest? I doubt it; not for you:
you'll be too busy allocating harps!

My gift must be expendable
and yet should last
while it can still give pleasure:
a thought for you to gaze upon
that will make music in your mind
sing minstrel songs for you
and ring you bells.

I have the very thing, and from Iona too!
You shall have my anthology of shells.

They have been washed by children,
counted, loved;
like you have travelled far, retained their beauty
still have tales to tell.
I'll put them in spring water in a glass,
and while you wait
for these sharp days to pass
I hope you may explore their colours,
hear their mysteries;
touch the green tears
that once a homesick St. Columba shed,
dreaming of Ireland, in his hermit's cell.

They bring you my goodbye and so much love.
I hope they shine out comfort
round your bed.

## Shall We Go Alternative?

I used to find it quite a rush
with Church and Sunday lunch
but now I go with New Age friends
to Meditation Brunch:
while we contemplate our navels
and eat Veggie Kedgeree
I pine for Bloody Marys
but there's only herbal tea.

We're learning Paneurythmy:
we go dancing every dawn
in our Barbours and green wellies
on a sacred stretch of lawn.
Next week we're starting classes
to 'heal the child within'
where you learn that feeling guilty
is a kind of New Age sin.

We can energise a Chakra
and see an aura flicker
which is certainly more thrilling
than a sermon from the Vicar.
We clank with Celtic crosses,
draped in bangles, beads and serapés,
we're blessed with many ailments
and are loving all the therapies.

I go for weekly channelling:
Burnt Feathers is my Guide –
in a previous incarnation
he says he was my bride.
He is very wise and holy
but it's well within his range
to give me helpful little hints
about the Stock Exchange.

Reflexology's as easy
as falling off a ladder:
you press the sole of someone's foot
to activate their bladder;
I'm trying Crystal Healing
and find that Acupressure
has done wonders for my sex life –
makes my husband so much fresher.

I subscribe to lots of Healing mags
and gobble up each issue,
I never leave the house without
a charged up Kleenex tissue;
I book on every Shrine crawl
as I'm hooked on Holy Water,
when I've learnt to travel astrally
the journeys will be shorter;

but in Metamorphic Massage
as I toned my special note
I suddenly got smitten
by a streptococcal throat.
I *must* have penicillin
though it means committing perjury –
I'll say I'm at the Yoga class
and sneak off to the surgery!

## Behind Closed Doors

Was Beethoven put
in his wooden baby-cart
beneath a singing tree
learning from soft sounds
round this cradle
multiplication tables
in the murmuring leaves?
And did he store away for future use
an ABC of notes from thrushes' songs?

What was it like
to grow such giant symphonies
of experience in his ears
then pluck and harvest them
for us to hear?

Was deafness just the slamming
of a library door
to block out interference
of extraneous din
and concentrate complete attention
on the insistent miracle
at work within?

## Big-Game Hunting

I hide in paper forests
lurk by waterfalls
throw verbal lures
to elephants and tigers;
bait traps with rhyme and metre,
try free verse
and hope to catch
unwary dinosaurs perhaps,
or snatch a dragon
slumbering in its lair.

I'd like to call
a taxidermist in
to set my wild ideas
on wooden shields
to hang from hooks in little magazines
or decorate the walls
of new anthologies.

I try to snare
exotic creatures
with my honeyed lines,
or capture birds so rare
that they might cause
even an editor a small surprise,
then find with shame
the thoughts that flap about
inside the nets I've set
– already tame!

## Blackthorn

*(A song for William and Alice)*

I'll give my love a choir of stars
I'll give my love a cobweb dawn
I'll give my love a small brown bird
I'll give my love a thorn.

I'll give my love the singing stars
To light our eyes and charm our ears
And paint the music evergreen
To set us dancing down the years.

I'll give my love a cobweb dawn
So light and soft that in its folds
Our new-found closeness can be wrapped,
Kept first-light fresh but never cold.

I'll give my love a small brown bird
Of constancy to wing its way
Beside us through uncharted skies
And keep us steadfast day by day.

I'll give my love a blackthorn branch
Then if a cold north wind should blow
We could use its sharp spikes to spill
Warm memories on hard-hearted snow.

I'll give my love a choir of stars
I'll give my love a cobweb dawn
I'll give my love a small brown bird
I'll give my love a thorn.

## The Camomile Swan[1]

At first sight
nothing strange to see
except where curious furrows
marked a mower's route
around a summer field
whose yield was destined
for shampoo or herbal tea,
but aerial photography revealed
an unexpected migrant
hiding in the grass.

Did it preen feathered flowers
for secret solstice mission
who knows where?

Did it lift off
on wings of silence,
beak towards orange dawn
and silver tail to moon,
to spread an urgent message
through our troubled air?

If only legends
could be usefully recycled,
then a modern Zeus
might penetrate with love
a willing Leda, to father
not war-inspiring Helen
born of force,
but swans of peace
to fly our warring world!

[1]  Artist Simon English mowed a swan in a field of camomile for the Midsummer's
Day Solstice near Stratford-upon-Avon, photographs of which appeared in The
Times and several local newspapers.

## Cack-Handed
*(For Susannah with love)*

I wish I could pipe!

Oh I wish I could pipe.
Other people can do it
why can't I?
If I pipe a cushion
I know it will pucker
quite probably cry.

Arcadian shepherds
who lounge against rocks
looking prissily deft
blow rarified tunes
to their herbivore flocks.
But me? I can only blow
dandelion clocks.

If I pipe mashed potato
or worse still meringue
it causes my family
a panic alarm
as it sneaks from the bag
to creep up my arm
escaping the nozzle
with maniac jumps
to land round the kitchen
in sniggering lumps.

I wish I could pipe.

If only I could
I'd flute such green music
they'd all be beguiled
to drop what they're doing
and dance in the wild,
which would, sure-as-hell,
take their minds off whipped cream
and potatoes as well.

I've just had a thought:
pretty useless it seems
but there's one thing I can do...
pipe wonderful dreams!

## Caerhûn Church

A stillness of the spirit lies
inside these walls
like the strange lull that centres in a storm.
The chill of ancient worship wraps me round
as sunlight falls
across the silence, radiant but cold,
to fire the dust of sanctity with gold.

No flame of passion lights the candles now
yet to this place
men must have brought their agonies and griefs
come running here with bursting gratitude
for favours granted or a hidden grace,
to praise the God whom their great faith made real.

No doubt that silver fox Hypocrisy
has stalked this aisle
feasting upon the flesh of ignorance
with cruel teeth but sanctimonious smile.
But now no trace of bitterness remains
to spoil the light of this serenity
and here Man's inky passions leave no stain:
the brush of time has white-washed long ago
the sins that one time seemed indelible.

Where is the peace which passes understanding?
Is this cool calm
a freezing balm of partial anaesthesia
for bruised souls?
and is the quiet with which this air
is filled, the essence of much praying
now distilled?

Oh are you there, the God to whom they cried,
holding inside Yourself their fright and mine
waiting to cauterize with flames of love
the hate by which You are still
crucified?

## Wrong Number?

Still no reply –
God knows I've tried.
A voice keeps on repeating:
"The number you have dialled
is unobtainable. Please try later."

Perhaps he's moved?
Gone ex-directory?
Could I have pressed the mute?

My neighbour
has no trouble getting through:
*her* God sits with a cordless telephone,
just waiting for her calls;
she says he's never out at all
what's more, he isn't bored
by all her chat. What could be
more miraculous than that?

*Her* God recycles her opinions
wraps them up in sweetie papers
– she calls them 'Guidance' then
and sucks them all the time
but I get whiffs of peppermint
and think they may be humbugs.

He's always at her church:
she won't let him attend
the other ones, although I know
he pops off on the quiet
when she can't see.


I've spoken to the engineers:
they say communication's privatised.
If I insist that I must share a line
there's very little they're prepared to do.
it's just I'd really like to know...
*My God, where are You?*

## Fashion Page

If by ill chance
you have to wear a drab hairshirt
do not despair.
Accessorize
with chic and flair:
pin flowers on
or try a sequined sash,
shorten your hem and show defiant leg.
These garments can surprise
if worn with dash.

Sartorial warning:
this applies
if you already have one
in your wardrobe
for second-hand hair shirts
make dowdy dress.
A fashion tip to stress:
go wild, experiment,
transform the one you have,
but never trail the sales
deliberately to buy one!

# Catching Leaves

October sky
is full of rooks and leaves
and portents which I cannot read
– the only alphabet I learnt
just works for books.

I check to see that no-one looks,
then leap (ridiculous!)
and try to snatch
a lucky promise twirling from the trees,
or intercept
a fire-insurance voucher giddying
through the air.

They mock and flutter
swirling out of reach – but
would I use one well
if I should catch it?

Though strands of hair
breathe memories from lockets,
dried opportunities don't keep so well
in pockets.

## Cradle-Song

This year
we had a cradle
at the foot of our bed.

Oh, not the kind we used to have
where slumbering babies slept
securely wrapped,
but one that kept the bed-clothes
off your legs:
even the lightest sheet
put too much pressure
on your shell-thin feet.

Now you are gone
covers lie flat again
but the weight of your absence
is a blanket of heaviness.

I knew we had to part
and do rejoice
at your relief from pain,
but how I long to hear your voice –
that vibrant baritone
which often reached
further than you intended, for
you had no whisper.

I wish I had a cradle
to keep this grief
from pressing on my heart.

## Dust Storm

I have come to sit with you, Silence.

You snort, and twitch away.
Why choose today
when I have time for you,
to gallop off?
Your vanishing hooves
strike sparks of rage from my stone road.
I wanted you to stay and throw
a shawl of peace over my parrot cage
not kick your heels and go.

I ignored creased poems
on the ironing board
left stories simmering in the oven
unhooked my telephone
resisted books, refusing
all distractions just for you.
Are assignations only to be made
at your choosing?

When you creep unexpectedly
in training shoes to slide
your hand in mine
I do not hide from you:
you are a welcome guest.
Is it too much to ask
that you should sometimes come
at my request?

I came to sit with you, Silence.
A heckling wind arrived instead
and dust piles, stirred
by your departure, swirl
questions round my head.

## The Empty House

We tried to find
another way instead
but sometimes had to pass
a place where panic ambushed us
in tangled grass;
then my small daughter
clutched my hand and pressed her head
against my side.
"Real houses are alive,"
she used to say
"Don't let me see that unloved one
– it's dead."

Cancerous trees
sprouted from chimney ears,
a gaping jaw
swung on a broken hinge;
four lashless windows peered at us
through unbrushed bramble hair,
unblinking zombie eyes
blank as a blind man's stare.

We held our breath
and ran till we were past.
There were no sounds to cause such fear:
it was a silent song of hatred
we could hear.

Do those stone bones
still rattle skeletons and finger skirts?
I have not seen the place for many years;
perhaps it has been renovated now
given mod cons and made 'desirable'
...I only know
nothing would ever make me
buy that house.

## Far Cry
*(Remembering Amanda)*

A small blue flower grows inside my head.
It did not flourish in the flowerbed
where I first tried to plant it out
but in tight bud, still wrapped in early dew
it put down trembling roots and then withdrew.

Though hidden in my skull for twenty years
this ghostly plant blows echoes through my ear.
I may not hear its thirsty cry for months
or rake around its weedy patch, and yet
I can still water it, shall not forget.

## Flood Damage

      The river split its personality last week.

It rioted across the fields, swayed by mob-rule
and swollen with second-hand opinions
shouting obscenities, slashing at trees
eyes muddy with hate, quite beyond reason.

      My river, clear-eyed friend – a hostile stranger.

Yet I have often gazed at its calm face
and felt my own serenity restored,
or walked beside it hoping for advice
and heard its wisdom whispered in my ear.

      Tormented river, schizophrenic friend.

Last week it tossed all temperance to the wind
and spewed out ugly nightmares on the bank
where furious words that cannot soak away
have scattered hideous litter on the grass.

## The Frozen Congregation

Don't listen to the crying in the darkness
Don't let anybody know that you can hear.
Close your eyes to pain and desolation
And your heart to loneliness and fear.

Don't try to find the ones who are your neighbours:
You might not like the colour of their skin.
If you don't know anyone who is unwanted
There will surely be no call to ask them in.

Very quickly turn the pages of your paper
Lest your eye should fall again on that appeal:
If you do not see the picture of starvation
Then you cannot know that poverty is real.

Oh never let yourself become committed
It isn't always easy to retire;
If you do not stretch your hand to light a candle
You will not burn a finger in its fire.

If you are a frozen congregation
In your pleasure dome of ice you may remain
Sheltered from the sunlight of compassion:
A thaw might make you feel a little pain.

So stay in this icicle protection
Where your frightened little self can safely hide
But if anyone should try to crack it open


– They might find there is nothing left inside.

## James' Song

Oh did you volunteer to come
And how long will you stay
And can we learn enough of love
Before you slip away?

We greeted you with fear and grief
You seemed beyond our reach
But now we know a child of light
Who has so much to teach.

Sometimes you look with baffled eyes
Which fills our hearts with pain.
Oh is it that we are obtuse
And you cannot explain?

We march our roads with hustled tread
You step a different pace
But your path may be more direct
To reach your special place.

Oh did you volunteer to come
And how long will you stay
To teach us unconditional love
Before you go away?

## "The Grass Cathedral"
*(Engraved goblet by Laurence Whistler)*

Perhaps the boy
flat on his stomach in a summer field
paved with his poet's eye
an aisle through pillared stalks of grass,
whose feathery seeds
fan-vaulted invitations
in the sky.

One day
his glass-engraver's hand
would choose a medium for his skill
as fragile as a shattered window pane,
clear as transparent coverings of ice;
fleeting as roses flowering from clouds.

Choices:
always the choices lie
between the dark and light,
the blank wall, or the vista
which beckons teasingly,
but gives no guarantees.

Unseen moments
hide, shadowed in secret trees,
voices of angels
ringing out through glass,
soprano-cut and diamond bright,
spray canticles on star-spiced nights;
coffins ask questions, doors mouth messages

– and choices, always those choices
hang
between the darkness
and the light.


*This poem was inspired by the exhibition at Sothebys to celebrate Laurence Whistler's 80th birthday in 1992.*

# January 1991

Black ice coats motorways
to this New Year.

Dark thoughts of war
flap rook-like past a skyline
that has advanced too close;
for when far hills look near
all mountain people fear
the coming storm.

Weather reflects the news today:
even bright seagulls
have put out their lights
and are as hard to see in sleety air
as peace solutions
against desert sand.

So on this morning
I have lit a candle,
not in belief
that God will stretch a hand
through my closed windows
and snuff out the war,
for surely that is our
responsibility.

No, my small flame
flickers in anxious fellowship
for many mothers' grief.

## Jumping on Shadows

An afternoon
of raucous sun, unruly clouds:
I watch my children
playing tig with shadows
steering bright boats of laughter
to race their stretched black sails
across cut grass;
they chase and try to hold
a fleeting message down
with plimsolled feet.

If poems flicker secrets
through your brain
jump on their shadows quick
before the sun goes in.

## "Man and his Symbols"
*(A letter to Carl Gustav Jung)*

Walk with me through
this university of dreams
and guide my hand:
the papers are so hard
to understand;
the tutors masquerade
in strange disguise
juggle identities
wag unknown tongues;
books tantalize in code
and walls of lecture halls
dissolve and change.
Nothing is as it seems.

With syllabus so huge,
but term so short
I need a grant to live.
Interpret for me.
Stretch your hand
and place in mine a key
to all the secret archives
stored in me.

# Left-Hand Gloves

My cupboard has a shelf of left-hand gloves
Whose partners have been lost or thrown away:
The point of keeping them is hard to prove.

Though our twined fingers locked so close in love,
I saw your gauntlet buried yesterday.
Is there a use for one odd left-hand glove?

Your hand has gone that made our right glove move:
The glove became too thin for it to stay.
The point of keeping mine is hard to prove.

Two-handed, a bright tapestry we wove:
Now I must seek a different role to play
And find a use for just one left-hand glove.

I stretch my hand: is yours below, above?
And can you hear when I cry out and say
"The point of life alone seems hard to prove."

Your spirit's flown the body it once drove,
To find a subtler one, and I must pray
That I can find a use for one left glove –
Although just now the point seems hard to prove.

# Katie

The grown-ups called her Katie
– we called her Mrs Jones.

Rembrandt would have seen beauty
in her hunched and knotted bones,
mapped the fine pathways of experience
on her face; captured the shine
of gentle eyes and reproduced it
as a pool of light.

I thought it a wonder
that she had button shoes like mine.
In the mornings
she wore flowered overalls
(black for the afternoon
under a bibbed white apron, brisk with starch).

Sometimes she staggered under heavy trays.

She called us "cariad",
let us lick bowls and spoons
while we regaled her with the stop-press trivia
of our days;
she told us where to find
snakes-head fritillaries whispering
in the grass, knew where white violets grew
and taught us how
crushed dock-leaves can bring ease
to nettle stings on scrubby knees.
She laughed at jokes
listened to crotchet moans,
kissed bruises better when we made a fuss.

I wish that she could kiss me better now.

If she bubbled music in her mother-tongue
words were incomprehensible, and yet
always, we understood
the language of her love.
I hope that some of it rubbed off on us
for we shall not forget
dear Katie bach – whom we called Mrs Jones.

## Letter to a Surgeon
*(For Pam)*

First, grateful thanks from all her many friends –
too often broken things get thrown away:
toasters and fridges, dishwashers and irons,
"Cheaper to buy a new one," so they say,
and only treasures warrant careful mending:
rare porcelain, jewellery, and objets d'art.
How privileged you are! Under your care
you have had placed the precious outer case
of a most loving spirit – someone rare.
I know you have repaired her with much skill
and snipped and clamped to join with fine precision;
I like to think you also stitched with love –
she will heal so much quicker if you did.
Having such healing qualities herself
you too will get much blessing from the contact.
She was anaesthetized, you say and not aware?
Was quite unconscious? Oh but you cannot tell!
Her frame was out of action, that's a fact,
but where her spirit roamed, what she achieved
what intercession made, you do not know.
Healing can always be a two-way thing:
I hope so much you make each other well!

## Making Jam

They put love on a saucer
and hoped that it would set:
it did not wrinkle at their touch
and wasn't ready yet.

But young cooks are impatient
and not inclined to wait;
they poured it in a heated jar
marked with a marriage date.

They should have waited longer
before they sealed the pot
for sticky syrup, going off,
is all that they have got.

# Not Mincing Words

Today I shall cook mince.
I might even make jam
lash out, sew buttons on, but
I *am* going to cook mince.

I must lock all poems away:
they have become gluttons.
I shall shut them in my head
and turn the key.

Books sulk about on stairs
nagging to be read
or whinge for me
to put them onto shelves:
I wish they'd do it
for themselves!

Poems kick my door with furious feet:
I hear their screams
but take impervious stance
and go on chopping onions
browning mince.

Those verses have gone very quiet.
Suppose they overlay each other
like pigs and smother,
get my kiss of life too late?
Should I risk a quick look
not letting them see me
just peering through a crack?

What is that funny smell
I know so well? Burnt meat again!
*Oh Hell!*

## Missing Link
*(For Graham Rust)*

If I could paint like you
I'd daub my canvas with the roar of waves
which crash and suck on rocks
as they choke fury out on
brain-washed beaches;
I'd stipple sounds
of sun beating on sand,
and peer through Monet's half-closed eyes
to capture scents of orange groves at noon.

If only I could paint
I'd use a water-colour wash
to haze-in muffled hush of furtive mist,
borrow a pointed brush from medieval monks
to gild bright notes of birdsong;
define in pastel crayon
with soft lines, the cowslip whisper
of each morning's hopes;
splash laughter on my page
till colours run
kaleidoscoped.

If I could draw
I'd sketch the rasp and scrape
of winter twigs stabbing the wind,
and etch its shriek of pain
in black on white.

But I just think my images in words,
type printed pictures onto foolscap sheets
and have to understand
that, unlike you, I have no link
between my open eye
and disobliging hand.

## November

White horses terrorize the trees
stampede through grass with gold manes flowing
while wakes of seagulls keen their grief
to witness Autumn's violent going.

Power-driven branches beat the sky
and send a tattered army flying;
warriors of old might envy them
so beautiful and fierce their dying.

## Question Marks

Where certainties once lived
and laughter bred
now clouds of question marks
surround this house
rising and falling on each breath
of indecision,
mobiles of midges in my evening air.

The shadow of your absence
looms alarmingly
to flicker on my wall
while droning queries
buzz inside my ear,
changing in pitch but constant
in persistence,
naggingly asking
"Now you are gone
can I stay here alone?
Can I stay on – at all?"

## The Other Door

*(For Gemma Walker)*

I fly through my inner eye.

I leave the slow vibrating vehicle
parked in a chair: it is too cumbersome
and heavy for this flight.

I climb through rainbow terraces
and from each level must collect a leaf;
these are my vouchers for access to the summit:
if picked in hatred or resentfulness, they fade
and are no longer valid at the entrance.

The vista from the top is panoramic;
so many points of view lie stretched below
that I can only understand a few, and need a map.
There are supplies for travellers here
for everyone who comes must journey on.

A flock of silver birds wait for dispatch:
unlike ambiguous words, they carry
no misunderstanding on their wings.
Sent out in love, these carriers arrive
the moment they're released. There is no time lag.

I may bring others with me to this space
to drink the light and breathe the colours in.
They are not always people of my choosing
and I would often rather be alone
but if I lock them out, then I myself must leave.
Sometimes I long to linger and forget
the dusty engine that is left behind
although I know I am not ready yet.

Descent is fast. I fly back through my eye.

## Reflections

*(For D. with love)*

I faced about, met my own ghost,
it gazed at me bewildered, dumb
and challenged me with millpond eyes
to stare at what I have become.

It ventured close, stayed out of reach
singing of secret paths through trees.
I used to sing that song as well
till words blew off with childhood's breeze.

I sang to it of motorways
and passing in the outside lane:
it did not seem to understand
though I was desperate to explain.

I begged the-child-I-was, to stay
and promised it could still run free:
it backed away in mocking mist
and I was left ... alone with me.

## September Walk

Brush of stubble under my feet
and wind escaped in the trees;
scatter of finches at river's edge
hastily leaving the hawthorn hedge;
wide wing-span of a heron's flight,
flapping nonchalant, out of sight:
let me give thanks for these;
oh let me give thanks for these.

Shop-lifting pigeons palm the corn,
thistledown's broken free;
as scimitar swallows slice the sky
they are sharp with joy, and so am I:
sun is a lover's touch on my face
and the rock in my heart has a resting place:
long may the memory stay with me;
long may it stay with me.

The river carrying yesterday's rain
express to expectant seas
is brown with peat from moorland streams
and silt from all my outmoded dreams;
green and gold will soon be dispelled
for summer and ecstasy cannot be held –
but may I remember these,
oh may I remember these!

## Sparrows

They have small claim to fame
though one was once an epaulette
on Thoreau's shoulder;
they get a mention in both Shakespeare
and the Psalms – though what does not? –
but not too many odes
from other bards;
nothing in Hansard, Who's Who, or Debrett
for cheeky peckers-up of gossip crumbs
in small back-yards.

They never warble
with high Anglicans and larks
or bubble lullabys in moonlit groves:
they do not really sing at all
just chirp sharp cockney jokes
in rhyming slang
round city parks.

They play no top league games
with swans and peacocks
don't dye their plumage purple
for mohican crests
or sport banana beaks as toucans do;
they look their best
dressed in old vests
and tatty cardigans
while they play hopscotch with their mates
down narrow streets.

Feathery feeders of opinion polls
small riders on the Clapham Omnibus
safe birds-next-door:
stay with us – sparrows!

## Skimmed Milk

Llichan Ucha: liquid name of farm
where hand in hand we went
for milk. The dairy smells
of slate-slabbed cleanliness
and chilling rectitude in chapel pews.

Mrs Owen blows the fat aside
scoops pale blue fluid up
and fills our can;
if we are sent
for cream, immoral thought,
she skims it off the pan
with surreptitious dips
into the blue below
then tips it in our fluted jar
for luxury should be diluted so.

Mr Owen cannot smile
in case his waxed moustaches crack.
a parcel tightly tied with string,
cords below knees and elbows,
is he afraid that fantasies may weave
up trouser leg or sleeve
and make him sin?
Did Mrs Owen on their wedding day
rip all the wrappings off
to peep inside?

Did they find love
in their great feather bed
or copulate for procreation's sake,
a Biblical pursuit and thus allowed?
Before he bound himself with knots
against the wicked dew,
perhaps he blew
the cream off her teetotal head
and filled her veins
with thin skimmed milk
instead?

## Swing-Song

*(A chant for children)*

Bird-singing children chant to and fro
"Swing me over the apple tree, Joe."
Buckets of laughter, pockets of hope
Wonderland wings with a swing on a rope.

Straighten the legs then bend the knees
Sail off with swallows over the trees
To and fro, to and fro
"Push me harder!" "Over you go!"

Feet in the air and head in the grass
Daisies and dandelions swishing past
Flowers for a hat and sky for a shoe
Skim with dragonflies into the blue.

"Don't stop pushing I've just begun
Swing me higher, beyond the sun!"
Over the branches, jump if you dare,
Into your daydreams, and disappear.

## Thinning Grapes

I teeter
on a rickety top step
to reach a bunch of grapes
then clip my way into green jungle
to vent its dense interior,
letting in light and leaving
room for growth.

Pointed black scissors
have hung on this vinery door
for a hundred years or more,
my fingers the latest
in a long lineage of pruners' hands
to nip unwanted berries out.

Snip snap snip snap
bright moments drop upon the floor
to shrivel into wrinkled memories
– the scissors that thin my life
are not only dark and sharp
but I do not know who wields them.

My ladder shakes with doubts.

# Waiting

Two birds are circling in my skies:
the nightingale of yesterday
the condor of tomorrow.

How far away that bird of May!
How hard to catch the notes it sings!
But dark and close the bird of prey
whose ghost-train feathers brush my eyes!
This vulture waits to pick the bones
and feast upon red meat of sorrow.

But oh, the bird that is today
where is its song, where are its wings?

## Watching Seals

What a spoof!
How miraculous, this
sleight of hand design!

First the disguise –
as part of rocky outcrops in
the grey Atlantic surge, next

pretence –
the lumpish drag of handicap,
as weighty flesh is heaved
on hopeless limbs, then

SPLASH!
The shock of elegance,
of streamlined power and pace;
aquatic ballet, ocean-splitting grace

– and I could watch
this conjuring trick all day!

## The Doctor's Dilemma

*(A cautionary tale for conservationists. For Geoffrey Hall)*

I specialize in lupins
They're my pride and my delight
I fertilize and water them,
Converse with them each night;
They win me many prizes
They're the glory of my life
When I show them to my neighbours
And share them with my wife.

I look at all this beauty
That God and I have made
(I buy the seed, He made the earth,
I dig it with my spade)
And while I dwell with pleasure
On our joint co-operation
I look upon my flower-beds
With awful consternation:
For my very special lupins
In the bed which I have dug
Have been *absolutely ruined*
By a hungry burgling slug.

I've always felt that there is room
On Earth for one and all
To live in perfect harmony
Along with Dr. Hall
So I tell the slugs I love them
And am pleased that they should dine
But I also tell them firmly
That the flowers *are solely mine*!
I go to bed quite happy,
Feel I dealt well with this matter
But next day my lupins look much worse
And all the slugs are fatter.

I pile the slugs in flower-pots
And take them far away
And instruct them, very kindly,
That this is where they stay.
I know that I have treated them
As fairly as I could
But slugs are very greedy,
And the taste of lupin, good:
The minute that I leave them
They require a tasty snack
And by the time I'm home again,
The slugs are also back.

This time I'm very angry,
To a Garden Centre drive
And intend that pretty shortly
There will be no slugs alive:
I say I wish to purchase
A really lethal pellet
And the Garden Centre stock one
And are very keen to sell it.
Now I spend my days in healing
And cure the sick and ill
But suddenly I wonder
If a doctor ought to kill?

I see those lovely lupins
In the bed which I have dug
But question: are they *meant for me*
Or are they *for the slug*?
I ponder on the matter
Of God's manifold creation
And decide perhaps the slugs and I
Should go to Arbitration.

## Widow's Weeds

My Gardener has gone
and gatecrashing goosegrass
seethes over ground he once tended
strangling the light.

Milky-fat thistles,
oozing self-pity,
suck all frivolity from earth
and starve the bright flowers
that he loved
of life and laughter.

Fierce nettles march
to commandeer my once-calm lawn:
our secret spring is choked up
and my viewpoint is obscured
by brambles.

Beware, beware,
hateful encroaching weeds
for I can learn to wield a knife!

You shall not take this garden over.
I will put on leather gloves
and root you out.

# Dowsing

Cut me a hazel twig,
Lord,
and grant me skill
to dowse for the Divine;
let me find
hidden prayers that ring
through unexpected things:

brave dandelions
which shine a torch
from tarmac cracks
to thrust their life-force
through resisting stone;

a packer at the check-out till
when I am tired
and energy has flown;

a sloughed off snake-skin
wrinkled with the past
reminding me to take a closer look
for somewhere secret, near,
a slithering new hope
may slide through grass;

that clump of cyclamen
I thought had gone;
the nut-hatch visiting
my window sill.

Cut me a hazel twig
and I shall understand
that You are there
– wherever its green suppleness
bends in my hand.

## Sinning the Mercies

My heart is full of fumes.
Cataracts obscure
the crocodile
of all my Blessings
which march past, two by two,
eyes right
saluting me.

I do not want to count them.

My spirits are encased
in plaster of Paris
and weigh a ton.
The Blessings, reproachful,
rush to write their names
across the cast – but
I will not read
their signatures:
there are so many, and –

I am ashamed.

## Mending Rainbows

Although my unripe gaze
fixed on the path I wished to tread
I feared to pass
the snarling challenge
tethered in my way,
so sidled off and took
a different route.

I should have gone
where I was looking – for
I tripped and fell
clutching my stock of rainbows
secretly.

I was relieved
they broke so silently
and no-one heard the crash
as shattered glass
rolled down the hill.

Now pausing further down the track
I see the scattered fragments
lying there
and start to wonder what I might yet do,
given a tube of courage
and some glue.

Is there an evening class
on mending rainbows?

## In the Dreaming

When we were in the Dreaming
a new scribble in God's eye
his angels scratched suggestions
on the land, for us to try.
Then God gave us identity
and breathed us into birth
till we danced along the guidelines
with reverence for the Earth.
We listened to its silence
read a message on the breeze,
understood the pulsing rhythms
of waterfalls and trees.
The resources of our planet
supplied our every need ...
until we raped and squandered them
with ruthlessness and greed.

Now ancient sacred pathways
are difficult to find:
they are hidden under motorways
where loaded lorries grind.
We've abused the holy places
by schism and dissent
and worshipped in a market
built of sequins and cement.
We have killed, polluted, tortured
spawned labyrinths of lies
and we may be very clever
but we surely are not wise.
We can split the smallest atom
keep scrap-yards up in Space ...
but we have not solved the problem
of the warring Human Race.

Once there were many stepping stones
which different men could tread:
for the truths of God are endless
as the stars above our heads.
The sickness of our bodies
shows bruising in our souls
for mind and heart and spirit
should be treated as a whole.
We must see again with inner eyes,
and hear with inner ears
to find a hidden wisdom
lest another Dreaming's near.
If we can search with urgency
we may not seek in vain ...
unless God takes another breath
and sucks us in again.

## Why Were You Born ...

You who could not stay
with us to share our life
which gave you breath,
and what is death
to those who have not lived?
What did you learn
who did not know man's love
or fear his scorn?
Why were you born?

So short your life
we hardly knew each other
never shared together,
songs or mirth:
only your birth
I shared before a bleak goodbye.
What spark survives
or were those few fraught weeks,
each day a knife,
your only life?

Where are you now
and can I find you
on the road through life
that I must tread,
or are you dead
that have not sinned
or sacrificed or laughed?
And shall I search for you?
Oh tell me how!

Oh tell me
          how.

## Meditation on Apple Trees

When dank depression
wreathes a sulphurous smog
around your clogged up heart
inhale a thought to breathe its fog away,
for who can think of apple trees
and still feel grey?

Surely there's hope
if arthritic limbs can flourish
unfailing each Spring
in such frothed resurrection of blossom?

O Praise! Jubilate!
Come Let Us Sing! Abandon despair
for the morning-star ring
of each fruitful variety's name
– Ribston-Pippin, Cox-Orange and Russet!

Each juice-running bite
spurts pleasure of sunshine and Summer,
or dark mossy smells
from apple lofts guarding their treasure
for the toe of a child's Christmas stocking.

Store apples on shelves in your mind
for crunching on dark days of doubt,
then fling open shutters of gloom
– dance out to an orchard of light!

## In Memoriam

You do not need memorials of brass
on cold church walls:
your name is written on the wind-streaked sky
over the open moors
where red-grouse call.

I do not want your epitaph on stone
carved round a tomb:
your story can be read in flowers and shrubs
and those rare trees you planted
round our home.

I shall not hoard mementoes in a box
with plaque inlaid:
your spirit will live on while I can keep
green memories of the garden
that you made.